Where Are the Meek?

Presumptuous Laws,
The Alchemy of Money and Interest...
And Other Essays

WHERE ARE THE MEEK?

Where Are the Meek?

Presumptuous Laws,
The Alchemy of Money and Interest...
And Other Essays

Barry Leonardini

Library of Congress Control Number: 2003090918

ISBN: 0-9728416-0-1

Manufactured in the U.S.A.

Fresh Clean Day Publishing

www.freshcleanday.com

Contents

INTRODUCTION

The grizzled old warrior astride his war horse on the cover of this book is the incarnation of the subject matter covered in these essays. Where is he going? What is he up to? Has he thought it out? Has he thought too much? Just one more season? This could well be his last.

This old warrior has never seen a natural law or natural setting that he didn't change to fit his purpose. This includes taking laws and dynamics of nature out of their evolutionary context and modeling sophisticated tools, which include genetic engineering.

He created a detailed language and also created money. With these tools he has constructed and enforced, through monetary means, detailed laws that are mostly at odds with natural law. Man dictates equality in a cosmos known by its differences.

He is also a colonial. He spreads the doctrine of democracy which is the engine of consumerism. Our domestic colonials are hyphenated American citizens and other legally created classes of equals.

In these examples, the reason for his behavior can be traced to his heritage of homo habilis – the tool making man. We are supposed to have evolved into homo sapiens – the wise man. But I think the jury is out on that self proclamation.

The Empirical and scientific evidence shows this struggling against his natural lot in life has only ensnared him more deeply in the grip of the natural world. The care and maintenance of his tools, which include money and language, has made man the least efficient species on the planet. He is as effective as his power supply.

I would hope that these essays would engage the reader to compare codified behavior with natural law. The object of comparison would be to close the gap between man's law and natural law. Also, the essays suggest that a less mechanized approach to the pursuit of one's life would be more personally rewarding.

WHERE ARE THE MEEK?

ESSAY ONE

WHERE ARE THE MEEK?

WHERE ARE THE MEEK?

In ancient Rome, the Christians and the Jews were put to death under gruesome conditions on the floor of the Roman Coliseum. How things have changed! Rome fell because of its untenable colonial network of support. It has been succeeded by democracies in the West which have the Judeo-Christian ethic as their manifesto, i.e., all are equal because God said so. From putting to death arbitrarily anyone who challenged Rome's authority, we have evolved a legal system that makes justice an increasingly delayed or absent affair – no matter what the crime.

There is more money in the practice and posturing of law than real time justice.

Equality. That one undefinable word in the hands of politicians, judges, lawyers and bureaucrats has expanded to create new legal classes of people with codified subsets. Equal rights now include gender, race, religion, age and sexual issues including... sex change operations. It is a dynamic process of continually equalling down, never equalling up. Democracy is a degenerating experience. The bible claims "the meek shall inherit the earth." Where are the meek? Our domestically raised citizens have been joined by the flood of immigrants that continue since our founding to create a nation of colonials. Our founding fathers largely eradicated the indigenous population and placed the remaining Indians on reservations. So, I guess we can say that this is our home and we are now indigenous because of possession. But because our legal system is based on equality, which did not obviously apply to the Indians at that time, we have become legalistic in our relations – political correctness being the pop form. We have become quasi-colonials with hyphenated race descriptions (the Indians must be amused). The hyphenated citizens include all the extracts from Europe and other continents: French-American, Irish-American, Spanish-American, African-Americans, Chinese-Americans, etc. Then there are the subsets based on sex. These are the gays. I must say gay is not a description that I would use to describe a group based on sexual preference.

Equality has turned into special equality. How much special interest legislation can a country have before the country ceases to be a cohesive entity? Who will fight for the country? Wars are about endurance – who will endure? When a citizen in a country loses goodwill towards his fellow citizen, how long before a break up will come in the country? Goodwill ceases when legally mandated equity systems are put in place. Affirmative Action, transfer of wealth, political correctness, individually are a basis for instability in the country but together make it inevitable and irresistible. Our wealth divided by increasing classes of people make equality more and more of a luxury. Why did it work here for so long? It really only worked here prior to the 1960s. There are exceptions – tax code, etc. But the 1960s brought in a sea change of new legal definitions. It was similar to Attila the Hun forcing Rome to supplicate and make an enclave out of an Empire. But this time it is a different spelling of Attila. This one is spelled A.T.L.A. (American Trial Lawyers Association) and HUNdreds of laws. Social equity laws have become a full employment act in the redistribution of all that matters – personal choice, local schools, product of work, etc. Money makes lawyers and politicians able to operate. Without money, these synthetic classifications would go away because no one would pursue them. One wonders, since we are hyphenating our race origins in America now, should the Europeans have stayed home? Is racism or ethnocentric identification a natural way of living that cannot be suffocated? What I mean by racism is the preference shown by people to associate with like people. What's wrong with that? Rand McNally and other cartographers came into existence following the distribution and settling of mankind.

Will America break up into raced-based enclaves with symbiotic exceptions? I believe it will. Wealth holds our democracy together. Goodwill cannot be bought. Goodwill is what is needed. Sustainability should be the test or question asked of the philosophy of government. Colonialism, in whatever form, is not sustainable. Once you codify race relations, that is the seminal moment for distortion of relations for profit. One of the reasons that software and computers have done so well is because the litigation problem of equality issues goes away. There is no race, religion, sex, nothing. Only the ability to work the computer is required.

Our foreign policy has certainly changed since the caveat of George Washington "beware of foreign entanglements." We have become the messianic juggernaut of democratic nation building whether anyone wants it or not. It is a fact that democracies are great engines of consumerism. It is still colonialism, but a little more subtle.

President Eisenhower warned of a "military-industrial complex." Events in Kosovo, with NATO unilaterally declaring war on a European state no larger than the State of Ohio, was a sea change for modern day western civilization. This was clear aggression. Preventing genocide was the name of our Trojan Horse. The real reason ranged from a Monica Lewinski cover-up to a New World order gambit. Maybe the New World Order includes bombing improved real estate so that repairs can be done. Democracies cannot function without money. Money cannot exist without interest rates and interest rates are only collectable if growth is happening. I think the American people are crusaders in a kind of genocide. This kind of genocide is aimed at people who have their own idea on how to run their country and don't want to put it to a world vote. We have declared that there is no better way of organizing a society than to have democracies. And if you don't listen to us, we will find a way to bomb you. They said there were 37,000 sorties of fighter bombers from NATO into Kosovo – that is outrageous.

Kosovo shows the basic bias of indigenous people to their own kind and repugnance to colonials or invaders. The Ottoman Empire invaded and won a battle in Kosovo over 400 years ago. They established a colony. They were Muslims. They were from a different background and culture. Kosovo was not native to them. Ever since that time there has been racial friction in that country. America with NATO come along and take sides. We solved nothing in Kosovo. We and NATO have made new enemies. No small part of the New York September 11, 2001 episode could be traced to the West's arrogance in Kosovo.

The West has been meddling in the Middle East since the search for the Holy Grail by the Crusaders. The creation of the state of Israel by the U.N. in 1947 at the expense of the Palestinians was arrogance of Homeric proportions. Israel is now the colonial in the Middle East. The indigenous Palestinians are naturally unsympathetic to their presence. Israel's position is unsustainable. Hopefully, we can distance ourselves from that country and not be dragged deeper into their troubled vortex.

The famous political quip that all "politics are local" is correct. Whatever biases that exist around the world are not our affair. Everyone has bias. It is also called by another name: critical thinking. We cannot submerge critical thinking forever. It is akin to holding a blimp underwater. It can't be done for long. The U.N. and NATO are just as aggressive and greedy and colonial as Caesar or Hitler. Bias and prejudice around the world, or in this country, must be ignored. Any codification of personal taste is both impossible because of a lack of definition and unenforceable because of its ubiquity. Any micro managing will need the apparatus of a global totalitarian state and, in the end, will fail anyway.

WHERE ARE THE MEEK?

ESSAY TWO

WHERE ARE THE MEEK?

THE ALCHEMY OF MONEY
AND INTEREST

The traditional story of the Island of Manhattan was that the Indians sold it to the newly arrived colonists for some beads and trinkets. That was a type of monetary transaction. Beads and trinkets have no intrinsic value. Our own paper money or coin has no intrinsic value, hence the monetary description. Obviously, the Indians did not get real value for their Island in the Hudson. It could be said with certainty that the trinkets did not improve their lives. The loss of their Island was an ominous precedent.

Meanwhile on the west coast, where the San Francisco Bay

Area is today, the Indians developed a monetary system based on abalone shells and trinkets – similar evolutionary steps are not necessarily local or race specific. A monetary system of abalone shells and trinkets followed their success with the bow and arrow and other hunting tools and hunting strategies. With the leisure afforded them by a well-stocked food supply, they created a monetary system. When they had everything that was vital for daily sustenance, then interest turned to entertainment and trinkets. This evolutionary step was logical. Why hunt personally if they could pay someone else to do it? The shells and trinkets of their monetary system changed the relationship they had with their environment and among themselves. Prior to their monetary system, they bartered among themselves. Value was strictly a personal judgment arrived at by the bartering parties, e.g., one portion of berries for a side of wild boar. Transactions of real value were consummated.

The monetary system changed all that. The work ethic was probably the first casualty, and the birth of politics can be traced to those money dealers. That was the beginning of the end for their culture.

Money is a tool. It came naturally for homo habilis – tool

making primates – to develop that tool. The colonists thought they were way ahead of the Indians intellectually. As it turned out they were dealing with equals. The Indians thought they made a good deal and the colonists knew they made a good deal. In retrospect, if one looks at Manhattan today, the world of the Indians had something to be said for it. The Indians had a sense of place and something to relate to. So in the end, we have gone full circle with the Indians. We have ended up making a bad finish to a good start, as the Indians made a bad finish to their good start. The common denominator of the transaction was money. The Indians replaced the basis of their culture with money.

The colonists made a world money center of Manhattan and covered the world with the paper currency of the United States. It is the reserve currency of the planet. Could the results of the evolution of man have turned out any differently? Could the creation of money by homo habilis have been avoided? The answer is no. Tool making apes were bound to invent money. It is a predictable evolutionary step when the goal of tool making apes is to make the most ubiquitous, all in one, handy-dandy tool for whatever their frivolous primate heart desires. But it had a cost. Diverse people, literally from distant points on the globe, made the same error in replacing their cultures and work ethic with money.

Can we learn? Where do we go from here?

Natural assets have to be valued at their intrinsic worth or they will disappear and us with them. We need a barter system. It would result in better sustainability and give everyone a sense of place. The environmental movement has evolved as a result of the excesses of a monetary system, but we still use money as a medium of exchange and, by definition, trade paper or coin for living and personal natural resources. Another fact is pulling us toward the barter system. We are replacing ourselves with our own tools. Our personal labor is being demonetized with machinery. With the evolution of our ancestors, sophisticated work saving tools evolved. Included in those tools were language and money. Consequently, the percentage of actual personal physical effort steadily went down as a percentage of a work project – the machine was the effective tool and the human guided its path.

Money and our advanced logistic capabilities allow man to take advantage of disparities in wages and availability of natural assets around the world. We manufacture offshore and import other nations' natural assets more and more. Our high standard of living requires cheap labor. Somebody always has to be a slave. We finance the cheap labor with national and corporate debt that have rates of interest that require more cheap labor and more debt and so it goes. Growth is necessary to keep money valuable. Interest on money would disappear without growth. Money intrinsically is worthless. It has to be exchanged for something of worth for its value to be realized. We have a finite amount of natural assets, that do grow or evolve, but the more we draw down, the less we have to harvest. It is a zero sum game. Can we grow forever with other people's labor, borrowed money and limited natural assets?

Robert Malthus, the 18th Century economist, predicted the human species would end up duplicating itself into extinction. He could not have foretold of the efficiency of agra business, worldwide logistics and genetic engineering. Of course, everything else on the planet is in danger of going extinct in our place. Given enough time, Malthus may yet be correct.

A fallout of this transfer of wealth to our overseas vendors has been their plundering of other countries' natural assets. Some of the worst examples include the slaughter of rhinos, tigers and bears for aphrodisiacs and exotic medicine. One can trace our immense trade deficits by overlaying it on a map of the world which shows natural resource devastation. Money creates an exponential in human presence and influence. It allows humans to be in more than one place at one time. There are approximately six billion people on the planet, each having a control or say-so over a portion of the collective money supply. That exponential multiplies to an enormous munching jaw. Money also collects interest. This is a further exponential of the human influence. In terms of physics, the debt of nations would be similar to radioactive material that has a half life of influence on living things after the money has been spent. The interest collection ability of money is simply a form of alchemy. It lives, or radiates, 24 hours a day. We are all in debt because of the national debt. This is the reality of a monetary-based system. Our goal as a country is perpetual growth – we have to grow so that money remains valuable. We think about growth and debt more than anything else. Our country's motto should be "In Growth We Trust."

In the 1960s, First National City Bank and other money center banks created a new business model. Their thesis was that countries could not go bankrupt because of the wealth of their natural assets which were implicitly pledged as collateral. Therefore, they loaned huge amounts of money to Brazil and other South American countries. The Amazon jungle was reduced by ten percent to makeup the difference between the sustainable output of industry and the amount needed to pay back principal and interest. Simply, the nominal rate of interest of the bank loan grew faster than the trees in the rain forest.

The influence of money is also a form of colonialism. It is an export of another philosophical value. The most successful of all colonials was Rome and her efficient armies. The expansion of the Roman Empire was facilitated by the Roman Army and their conquests. Peoples were conquered and then enslaved, and the lands were stripped of their natural resources. These resources financed the Roman life-style and other conquests. But colonialism is unsustainable as history has shown. In the end, the colonials have to go home. The conquered sooner or later have nothing to loose – literally. They threw the colonials out and Rome had to learn a sustainable way of life for its own country.

That is roughly where America is at this moment. We have the largest money supply in existence and the strongest currency because of our efficient processing capabilities of natural assets.

We also have a huge homegrown consumer market. But assets are running out. Because of their plunder and removal and they are also running out artificially because of environmental set asides and environmental laws. The dynamic of money growth plus interest plus population growth in exchange for natural resources leads us on a moribund course as a species.

It is our choice, we can live in a sustainable garden indefinitely or on a planet with a disappearing atmosphere. With a barter system, each country will have to look to its own resources as its only asset. If they loose those resources, they will literally loose their place on earth. Individuals will go back to a single influence or a single presence without money as an exponential. With a barter system, the individual who wants to fly like a bird, run faster than a cheetah and be stronger than an elephant, will have to put some effort into the virtual metamorphosis.

We can change now through a measured transition or wait until the global monetary system around the world collapses because of a lack of sustainable growth. If we don't change individually, locally and globally, we may end up with a barter system anyway. But the difference will be the form of government.

It may take the form of individual slave states or a worldwide totalitarian government. The assets of resources and labor will be usurped by the government. So the choice will be barter now or slavery later. This will be the ultimate battle on earth.

A worthwhile project would be a group of philanthropic foundations, because of the tax status, joining together to set up a pilot project of bartered transactions. One foundation might provide service, another might provide goods, with the third, both. There is nothing in society today that couldn't be done in a bartered society. The difference would be sustainability and efficiency. Skills would emerge more quickly. The divisions of labor would recede and with it the blunting of creative impulse.

Does it all sound farfetched? If someone spoke during the dawn of mankind and said that we're going to loose our place to paper money, that would have sounded equally farfetched. It is up to us to find a way to live that is both sustainable and rewarding, these are inseparable goals. We fall well short of these goals. The rewarding part has been replaced by the pursuit of novelty and the sustainable has been replaced by the pursuit of convenience.

So we revert to a barter system and sustainability is achieved.

Would that stop us from starting up a monetary system sometime in the future? No. We could make the same mistake again. This plan buys us some time that we wouldn't have, given the present course. Our species will probably not last as long as we have already. Maybe in the end we will become the small primate again, but this time the tool making ability will be erased because it was unsustainable and not appropriate.

ESSAY THREE

WHERE ARE THE MEEK?

The Moment Is All We Have

There is only change. Time is a fiction. If nothing existed then there would be no change. If there is no change then there is no time to track that change. Time is our idea and creation - change is the metaphysics of organisms.

Einstein postulated that nothing in the universe travels faster than the speed of light. I think change is certainly as fast, but probably faster, than the speed of light. This explains action at a distance. Change virtually eliminates distance. Light is a secondary result of a work in progress. Wood burning gives off light. The sun burns hydrogen and gives off heat and light, but the light is only a telltale of the combustion that preceded it. For light to go faster than the combustion would violate the conservation of energy principle. If change is the fastest rate, then we are personally as fast as anything in the universe. This fact may add a measure of personal place and peace.

Nunc ipsum. This is a Latin phrase that means "only the present." That is all anybody ever had and all we will ever have. So if someone speculates when was the best time to live, the only answer that one could say is now. Because we are alive now. Of course, if one would like to speculate as to what period one would liked to have lived, that is available now more than ever. Hindsight is always 20/20. Speculating on how an individual might have coped during a specific historical era would be just that – speculation. Circumstances and heredity make up an individuals' behavior. To judge that one would be better off at a different epoch in history is a moot point. They would have had to have been there and, of course, that is impossible. The exercise of what to do in the future is a now event. Nunc ipsum is always the starting point. That comes from our very special ability to control change and by extension, the fiction of time. But do we really control change? We can certainly affect the landscape with machinery and, on occasion, weapons of destruction. We can certainly have an impact on disease and help people live longer. But in both cases we borrow from tomorrow to get through today.

In the case of antibiotics, we literally give the medicine away to anyone in need – both in America and around the world. I have undergone operations and would probably not be here if not for antibiotics. I think that my experience is shared by at least half the people on the earth. Antibiotics save lives. They also contribute to overpopulation. We humans play at creation and will pay for it later. So we have, in fact, lost control of change.

Recently, the Bill and Melinda Gates Foundation dedicated millions of dollars to the eradication of sleeping sickness in Africa. Sleeping sickness has been a problem in that country since time immemorial. It has gotten worse in absolute terms because of the growth in population (aided by the West's outreach programs). In relative terms it is about the same. The well-meaning but naive Gates family with their enormous wealth, has decided to eradicate this disease with free drugs and consultation.

Where will all the people live who have been saved? What

will they eat and how much? Who will counsel them with respect to their new challenges? There is a Chinese proverb, "When you save a life, you become responsible for that life." Will the Gates family leave a web address for future assistance? Over the millennia, Africans have developed some resistance to this sleeping sickness in their blood makeup. It is called a sickle cell. This is the same cell that causes problems for Africans in other environments.

Technology multiplied by money is mutually exclusive with peaceful, sustainable living – constant change is the result of that dynamic and by definition constant change means chaos.

The big difference of money will, in the future, diminish because of the total tab of the inefficiencies of a monetary system. All foreign aid and, for that matter, all domestic transfers of wealth and healthcare initiatives should be accompanied with an environmental impact study. With the disappearance of money, we will see how much real charity and care giving is appropriate.

Nunc ipsum does hold some benefits for man if he is willing to learn with critical judgment. Of all the sciences to study now, anthropology is the most timely. The results of locating, analyzing and dating traces of human habitation and its greater influence, are readily available.

Our ancestors branched off a common ancestor which included the gorilla and chimpanzee. We share 99.6% of the DNA configuration of the chimp. How did we turn out so differently? Because we multiplied that tiny difference by approximately two million years. A lot can happen to a ship that changes its original course for two million years. There are a number of well documented and very well written books on the subject of anthropology and paleontology. They all describe the same equation. The ascent of man means the descent of most other species and land diversity. It is a tale of extinction and land degradation. This is a zero sum planet. The study of this science builds a case for misanthropy. The scientists that wrote the books had no strong conclusion on the negative impact of the human species. The conclusions or advice they put forward ranged from no comment, to better surveillance of the rain forest, to colonizing other planets with the use of a passing asteroid. Nobody mentioned a frivolous primate with an inappropriate ability – sophisticated tools. So with nunc ipsum and the 20/20 hindsight provided by the research of the frivolous primate, there are some positive steps to be taken to mitigate a misanthropic view.

The problem is, nunc ipsum, is never enough! Man has never reconciled that fact. There is some justification. Even animals have to plan ahead. But they plan at a more instinctive level. Consequently, they probably fret less and have less circumstances happen that create paranoia. They get more out of simple circumstances. The outside world is their home, which is a luxury when all things are considered. Time and money are two of mans' primary tools. "Time is money" is a familiar quip. The quip also has a sense of urgency or impetus to agitation. Planning according to time is more of a conscious act. Planning according to need is more of an instinctive, unconscious act. It takes less energy. So, we have evolved to a point where we have piled one tool on top of another. Sometimes we have a tough time personally reconciling ourselves to their mandates. Timekeeping is how we keep up with society. Money is how we interact. Time and money by definition lead us away from our own present, nunc ipsum. They lead us away from the only thing we ever had or anything that we will ever have. There is justification for planning ahead. But there is equal or more justification to making the most of the moment. That requires a quiet mind at peace in one's own company – able to think things through.

Blaise Pascal, a French scientist and philosopher, commented on the Western mind as "not being content in an empty room." Time and money have lured us out of the present with the idea that change would be better. A pursuit of novelty would be rewarding. There is a Chinese curse that goes, "May you live in changing times." There is more money in circulation now than ever before. It covers the globe. Governments, through their taxing ability, have the most power to change. Big government and small minds are the problem.

WHERE ARE THE MEEK?

ESSAY FOUR

WHERE ARE THE MEEK?

Use a Tool, Loose Your Place

Heraclitus, a 6th Century B.C. Greek Philosopher, summarized, "All is flux." Change is constant. Newton summarized that gravity was the organizing force of that flux. The changes of the universe were understandable in the light of gravitational influence. The gravitational interplay of our own planet and our sun and moon with our molten core influenced the distribution of life on our planet. Trees will grow just so high, mountains have a limited elevation and flora and fauna will distribute themselves based on those general gravitational laws and the particular subset of specie specific physical laws. Darwin further defined a natural selection dynamic.

Along comes man after four billion years of planetary evolution. Ever since one of our ancestors picked up a stick in self defense (necessity is the mother of invention) and used its lever potential, we were never the same nor was the planet. Our species of ape was a sport on the evolutionary tree (we have a bicameral brain). We grabbed the stick knowing intuitively of the advantage it gave us. The club could also be used offensively. It aided in our killing of other animals for food and sport, which facilitated our security and population growth. It also gave us more leisure time and the ability to wage war on a new mechanized level.

With leisure time and our unique ability to focus and analyze, we observed other dynamics, mechanisms and systems that occurred naturally in our surroundings. We took their essence out of their evolutionary context and modeled sophisticated tools that could be exploited by us. That is our blessing and our curse. The blessing is the ability to mimic natural dynamics with tools – levers, pumps, combustion machines. The curse is we take them out of their evolutionary context and cause imbalances –

bulldozing natural landscapes, using the power of the atom for mass destruction, exploiting the use of antibiotics which contributes to overpopulation. I know we can't walk without leaving a footprint, but we have moved far beyond that modest step. These tools changed our relationship with the earth and all living things. What was natural became debatable. It could be changed. With this change in attitude, we assumed the role of creator.

Prior to our species, organic evolution was the creator and sculptor of our earth. Things and animals changed over long periods of time except when the occasional meteor rearranged the landscape. With the decline of the dinosaur, mammals went into an ascendancy. With our species, mechanical evolution took a heavy hand.

Natural selection is a manifestation of the physical laws of our planet. Since we are mammals, we are the incarnation of those physical laws and are bound by their directives. Of course, we could do things that are not prudent, we do have a free will, but we pay a price, e.g., eat too much and become fat, build too high a building and invite collapse, subsidize problems and watch them grow.

We have escaped our planet's gravitational pull and have visited other planets. But what part of our culture would benefit aliens? Will we learn to have peace of mind by interstellar traveling, or will we just introduce exhaust fumes into the void of space and find that no matter where we go, we are still there. If we colonize the universe in the fashion we have colonized the earth, who will welcome us?

Will man's tool-making ability ultimately cost him his place on the earth? Where does he stand now and in the future? Mulholland, the engineer who piped water from the Owens Valley into the arid area that was to become the greater Los Angeles sprawl said, "We are doomed by our success."

Soon after we started using tools, our primitive communications changed. A more sophisticated and complex language developed which included the written word. Our sophisticated language could only develop by having our daily burden of survival lifted by the use of tools. One does not have the energy or presence of mind to speak when hard work is being done. The spoken and written word became the foundation for our modern species. We went from homo habilis to homo sapien – at least nominally. We went from personally applying ourselves to work projects, to using machinery, to the development of software to run computers to run the machinery. We have become somewhat superfluous. We have become mere consumers. Someone to use the products of the machine.

How do you stop man from using tools? You can't. You can only mitigate the effects of technology. Critical thinking must be brought back into the school curriculum and that includes changing the philosophies of how schools are run. Affirmative Action and all the social engineering laws should be eliminated if we are to truly educate people. Schools should be a local responsibility without federal intervention. Vouchers are high priced busing. Plato said if you understand the most basic or minute dynamic in the universe, you will be able to understand the extrapolation that is the universe. Instruct students how to analyze and organize facts that will give them the foundation to look for the metaphysics of any subject. They will find a similarity connecting all things. To have students memorize facts is a lot different than having them know and understand facts. Memorizing Johannes Kepler's laws concerning the revolution and periods of times of celestial bodies is a lot different than instructing how Kepler came to know these facts. Just because we know the culmination of Kepler's works doesn't mean we equal Kepler's personal knowledge. Kepler and other great minds understood much more than what was printed about them. In the end, that was the reward they earned for themselves on a daily basis. They did not need fame.

A law of physics – no work in, no product out. Memorizing facts can be done by machines and probably better. How to apply facts from disparate subjects to find a solution to another subject is what schooling should provide. Short of that, you are somebody else's creation. Facts at close quarters, or out of context, leave people with ambivalence or confusion. The proper distance to view facts should be the goal. Observe nature. Follow her example.

Our school system has degenerated into a political incubator. Revisionist historical data selectively presented to the individual student was the great coup of the Civil Rights activist. Our democracy has gone from Civil Laws that protect life and property to laws that dictate associative paradigms to the final insult of what can be taught and by extension, what students can think. Civil Rights laws that affect business are unfair. Businesses, clubs or any associations are still made up by people and should not be subject to someone else's tastes. The laws of our democracy read like a manual that is sent along with an appliance.

Critical thinking and the wisdom that follows must be taught and practiced. It will be the only way to mitigate the downside of a mechanized society.

A Chinese proverb states, "the beginning of wisdom starts by calling things their proper name." What would the Chinese philosopher call political correctness?

WHERE ARE THE MEEK?

ESSAY FIVE

WHERE ARE THE MEEK?

Democracy Is a Monetary System

Our democracy is really a monetary system. It has more to do with money than anything else. All other democracies have ended in monetary systems that couldn't be funded. Rome and Greece the most notable. Our monetary system is approaching the limits of the exchange of money for natural assets because of environmental and philosophical constraints. Failing that exchange, an alternative barter system will succeed, and with it, the country will gradually break up into individual informal states. These states will be made up of tribal-like families, groups or networks of preferred associates. "All politics are local" and there is nothing more local than one's family or group.

Politicians are caricatures of their constituents because they promise too much. And so the dumbest of the voters can understand the message. It also attracts the most informed, arrogant and aggressive of the voters with a "take no prisoners approach" to the opposing party. What naturally follows from these caricatures is the result that all governments are inherently unstable. Human relations are fragile on a one-on-one basis. The rhetoric of governments magnify tiny human relations to an inappropriate level. Perspective is lost and chaos is the result.

Our two most recent presidents are caricatures in the extreme. Clinton is easily the king of vulgarity. Bush is reminiscent of a Knight of the Order of St. George, crusaders in the 11th century. Bush should put the red cross symbol of that order on his limo.

There is a direct ratio to the size of government and the war, foreign or civil, that will certainly follow. The most effective and sustainable way for humans to live is in family or group associations. That is how we started. We have lived in that social form longer than under formal governments. We can still have our technology. Nobody can put that genie back in the bottle. But the exponential of money by fiat of the government will diminish its impact. One day it will become apparent that money will have to go because of the multiplying effect of the human influence it facilitates. The planet cannot accommodate the demand. Of course, taxes go also.

In its place, everyone will have to produce through a barter system. Natural law will succeed the entire legal system which is really a lawyer system. This means that there is more money in delaying and denying justice. The cost of our legal system is too expensive for a planet of finite resources to underwrite. Our legal codes exaggerate man's value. Philosophically speaking, returning to groups will be pretty simple. We are now a democracy made up of groups already. The so-called special interest groups or lobbyists are only tribes by another name. They all have ambition and will stop at nothing to grow their position. The inherent problem with lobbyists and special interest groups in a democracy is they have access to tax money. It is double representation. Without money the special interest groups' influence would be greatly reduced. The Civil Rights Act in 1960 was a classic special interest of the trial lawyers.

These laws mandated equality in a cosmos where inequality is the norm. We are all different. The laws diminished the basis of accountability of individual lives and capabilities. The events that led to those laws were local issues in the South. Those issues did not need a national fix. Ghandi-type non violent resistance would have worked better.

With a barter system in place, corporate welfare would also be eliminated. The lobbyists for timber companies who want access to national forests so they can clear-cut, would disappear. Price supports for dairy and commodities would cease. Both of these are abusive to the animals and the land. And there are many other examples. There are also lobbies and special interests that represent foreign countries. One of those is the American Israel Public Affairs Committee. This group is partly enabled by the money grant it receives from the United States. They receive approximately $3 billion a year. President Carter and his Camp David accord instituted the cash grant in 1980. Egypt also gets $2 billion a year. Basically, they were bribed by Carter not to fight each other. Clearly an unsustainable foreign policy. The area is more dangerous now than ever before. The Israelis, through their locally paid representatives, are enabled to buy additional influence in Congress and in legislatures across the land. This is truly an egregious example of double dipping and not what the naive Carter had in mind. Our relation with Israel has always been a one-sided affair. Israel was the beneficiary... we got nothing. The latest negative return was the September 11, 2001 catastrophe in New York. The event was based on our relationship with Israel. Israel was created out of Palestine. It is well known that the world's Jewry, through political influence and money, bought the votes in the United Nations to create their state and used America as the broker. No title search was done.

Today's government representatives are largely kennel raised politicians. They are backed by machine politics, which are driven by polls which are made up of opinions from dumbed down voters. It really means that the politicians are following their own recanted lies. The typical politician has rarely produced anything in the real world. A lot of them are attorneys who get paid more to create problems and delay justice. It is no wonder that the laws they pass reflect their terribly flawed way of life.

Our model of democracy came from the ancient Greeks. Then, when any politician for whatever reason aroused displeasure in the general population, pottery was broken and the name of the politician was inscribed on those broken shards. If there were enough shards, he was kicked out of the country. He was ostracized. "Ostra" was the Greek word for pottery.

Today, some might prefer a quick dispatch at the nearest curb. The ceremony would have few words, except that preceding the actual deed, a speaker would say, "It is for the children." When these caricatures pass the enormously expensive and misguided legislation, they always invoke the children. Well, we are all grown up and we didn't get what they said we were going to get, but we want them to "get theirs."

Most of the laws that our Congress has passed are quasi-genetic engineering experiments that don't work. The seminal fallacy of their philosophy is that "All Men Are Created Equal." That is not true. Trying to codify anything that is not modeled on natural law fails to the extent that it does not follow natural law. Only our synthetic monetary system holds the failed laws of our democracy together. In other words, people get paid to do the unnatural. How much law or charity will we have without money? It would still exist and be more effective. The job would get done because it would be sustainable. Whatever is given is what is deserved.

ESSAY SIX

WHERE ARE THE MEEK?

American Goals —
Domestic and Foreign

What is the goal of America? According to our leaders it is economic growth and equality. These are the same goals since our founding as a nation. The growth is becoming more labored as the scale of our size expands on a worldwide basis. The environment is groaning under the weight of our demand. Equality as an idea was theoretically possible in the beginning of our country. Then the horizons were limitless in their promise. Now that we have grown to fill those horizons, we have come face to face with our neighbors. There is an order of natural selection that will prevail. Equality is not possible.

Growth and equality, which were the engine and train pulling America forward, will become mutually exclusive as goals at some inflection point. Our highly refined generous and detailed definition of the care and feeding of equals becomes impossible when it requires another huge quantum of economic growth to fund it. Politically speaking, the democratic party has thrived on the equality and environmental issues. That combination will be at a crossroads at some point - probably sooner rather than later. Social equity issues will end up with the short stick. Republicans were never onboard for those issues. The environmentalists picked up the equality activists partly by design and partly by default. But in the long run, the environment is far more important than equality issues.

Our domestic policies carry over into our foreign policy. One individual with the right tool can become an army of one. A few individuals with the right tools can change the course of history. I could be referring to the Manhattan Project of World War II. It fits that description. But there is a more recent Manhattan Project nicknamed 9/11. No nuclear bombs were used. There were only planes filled with topped-off gas tanks flown by people willing to give their lives for their cause. In a civilized nation a suicide bomber operates in a blind spot of the legal system. Our legal code is based on a commonwealth of citizens whom we assume are acting in a rational way in their pursuit of daily life. We cannot construct a legal code that is based on irrational citizens. They are the ultimate weapon given America's legal composition. As a country of laws, people have freedom of movement unless they commit a crime. In the case of the suicide bomber the law is broken when the plane is seized and then is compounded when the plane enters the building. Then it is too late. The most efficient bomber has included himself in the carnage thereby sparing America a trial. It is small compensation.

9/11 cost New York and the federal government approximately $95 billion. The airline industry basically went broke the following week and was bailed out by the federal government. Businesses have left New York never to return. As a country, we responded by bombing Afghanistan relentlessly. We lost some of our own men in friendly fire and killed many innocent bystanders. Afghanistan is not New York. Communications are poor. We bombed Afghanistan because of the alleged Taliban connection with Al Qaeda. Most people in Afghanistan never met Osama bin Laden or knew of the Al Qaeda plan for New York. The news flash on the subject was the flash of exploding bombs in their poor region. We created new anti-American feelings.

Now the President wants to unilaterally invade Iraq. He's gotten permission from the Congress. But the U.N. is opposed. Even our no-fly zone ally of Great Britain wants U.N. support before an invasion. The U.N. thinks we want to go too far.

We have gone too far. It is apparent that our foreign policy in that region is one that is based on the security of our oil supply and the security of Israel. The policy is ambiguous with one covering for the other in the political negotiating in Washington. The stakes have become increasingly higher in that region over the years. They have reached the point where a showdown is approaching. Will the Middle Eastern countries be able to determine their own future? Do they have sovereignty over their own countries? Or will the colonialism of the United States, Britain and Israel call the shots? The 1974 Arab oil embargo exposed our vulnerability. That is the reason why we should have pursued alternative fuels and alternative sources.

The region is unstable. That is the fact that does not give us the high horse of moral authority.

We have enforced a no fly zone over Iraq for 12 years. What is Iraq going to do that we won't see immediately? Iraq is supposed to have weapons of mass destruction. Well so do America, China, Britain, France, Russia, India, Pakistan, and Israel. We have been at odds or war with all those countries except Israel. Israel has about 100 nuclear warheads. No wonder the neighbors are arming. That count was taken years ago. A scientist in Israel was jailed for letting that information out. They supposedly stole uranium from a facility in Pennsylvania. Zionists are the soul of Israel. These racists are notoriously delusioned with their "God chosen" description. I think Israel is a bigger problem for America than any other country on the globe. The highest and best use of America is not protecting Israel. We should cut our losses with that country just as Carter did with Taiwan. The greater Islamic world is more valuable.

What an amazing story. An obscure Semetic tribe parlays a history of enslavement and genocide into a guilt trip for modern democracies. They used money and political influence to gather the votes in the United Nations to carve their country out of

Palestine and are enabled to run the United States' foreign policy by remote control with some of the money that the United States gives them on a yearly basis. Truly, democracies are a degenerating experience.

Times make the man. Leaders are followed from ad-hoc circumstances. Saddam Hussein is dangerous. We have him under a microscope. An invasion of Iraq is not necessary. Our dependency on oil created the cash flow which created that monster. We should get off oil. Osama bin Laden was also a beneficiary of our cash flow to Saudi Arabia. We should be proactive in our foreign policy and not reactionary. A proactive foreign policy in America would be one that generates goodwill. To that end, we should mind our own business. The suicide bombers and terrorist activity around the globe would stop. We should lead by example. That includes doing away with foreign aide and other covert attempts at nation building, which is really a code word for the advance of consumerism.

ESSAY SEVEN

WHERE ARE THE MEEK?

PRESUMPTUOUS LAWS

Werner Heisenberg was a 20th Century physicist. He postulated an uncertainty principle. The principle stated that when examining particles at the quantum level (the smallest unit of being) the monitoring process created a distortion that precluded a resolution of the position or speed of the particle. The process was too intrusive.

Is there a lesson for us in this principle? Does the principle scale up to man's level of consciousness and physical engagement in our own mental and physical world? Can we draw a comparison in lawmaking? Is there a distorting principle of bias that can be applied to writing less laws or in some cases, no laws at all? When we attempt to legislate equity laws in our society, we may preclude a just and workable law because of the self-interest bias of the group that is promoting the legislation. We often end up creating a bigger problem in consequence. The more we make laws, the more we define difference. The more the definition, the less the cohesiveness of our society.

The Civil Rights Act of the 1960s is that kind of legislation. They are presumptuous laws. It is impossible to outlaw bias because we all have bias. The fact that we exist means that we effect our surroundings. Any space that we occupy or situation that we are part of is unique because of our presence. Even when thinking by ourselves we can not separate our own experience or biases from the process of analyzing or planning. We are all different because of evolution. We all refract light, information and our environment differently. We all have a point of view, a way of life, a bias. Our own critical thinking is a must for survival. The possibilities of different opinions and relationships emerging from the common experience grows exponentially in the collective. It is also a zero sum process. What is gained or lost is offset by someone else's gain or loss.

As homo habilis – tool making primate, we developed language and the written word. One of the most ancient languages is Sanskrit. The literal translation of Sanskrit is "to make the same." That meant the characters on the paper or stone were supposed to be the "actual duplication" of the physical world object or event that one described. Describing and writing laws about behavior and social mandates and living by those laws are different by definition. Just because you can write a law into the Civil Code doesn't mean that it's appropriate or can be enforced. Laws only work if they are modeled on natural law. We are not all equal. Laws will fail to the extent that they deviate from natural law. Codified behavior came with the alleged evolution of homo sapiens – the wise primate. Laws concerning property rights and personal safety were the first areas to be addressed. As the power and wealth of society increased, so did the arrogance of the lawmakers. The Civil Rights of the early 1960s outlawed bias and codified personal taste. These laws can be compared to genetic engineering. Not the kind that deals chemically with our DNA, but potent nonetheless. The children who have been raised with the influence of the Civil Rights laws are hybrids of a human and a politically correct automaton. Rights have to be earned. Advantage comes from ability. All are not equal. This is the way the cosmos sorts itself out. We are known by our differences. Written laws will not override natural selection in the long run. The costs are too high. Our legal system only works because of money. Money has a limited future considering the costs involved in its exchange for human and natural assets. How we interact with people should be a matter of critical thinking and personal choice. The earth and its peoples are too broad and too diverse to write our own laws. We should learn from nature – we cannot direct it without unacceptable, long-term disadvantage. Nature doesn't really listen to us anyway.

Civil Rights laws and other social engineering laws should be repealed. They have failed on an academic level, SAT scores have gone down with their implementation and they have hobbled our society's ability to function on a sustainable basis. A repeal may avert the repeat of confrontation which gave them birth. But this time the agitators will be the people who want their critical thinking freedom back.

The landmark court case of Brown vs. Board of Education held that separate but equal was unconstitutional. The Civil

Rights Act promoted different but equal. The original problem of codified segregation sprang from arrogance. The codifying of the Civil Rights Act sprang from condescension.

We have replaced one extreme with another. How about everyone finding their own place?

WHERE ARE THE MEEK?

ESSAY EIGHT

WHERE ARE THE MEEK?

THE SLAVE GAP

America is a free country. Are we in search of slaves or low cost producers? Yes, we are. It is called offshore manufacturing. Every society that ever was or that ever will be has a slave-like part of their greater family. What qualifies one as a slave? The classic definition is when someone is owned by another. Our tax code owns us a certain portion of the year no matter what job we have. So, between the slave who works to produce a product and a slave who consumes that product, we are a slave state. To make up for any shortfall in "equality issues" that are mandated by the government, businesses find offshore manufacturers to fill in the slave gap. That works to a point. It is unsustainable. Politicians say democracy is the best plan for America and the world. We are ostensibly at odds with a totalitarian government. China is a totalitarian government. But we need them to make our democracy work. Our leaders continue promising more to their constituents. The promises are largely kept by offshore manufacturing. Offshore manufacturing also has a different incarnation – immigrant worker, legal or illegal.

Socialists or communist governments enslave their people and call it equality. The hierarchy of socialist and communist governments become the ruling cast. The point is, all forms of government need a low cost producer or an enslaved population – never mind the name they call it. Governments can only operate if there is production that can be taxed and redistributed.

America, which is approximately 4% of the world population, uses approximately 25% of the world's gross product. We are by that definition the ruling class of the world workers. Another way of looking at it would be that our democracy only works at that high a level of consumption by having someone else do work that we won't do or are prohibited from doing by our laws of equity or union code.

Does this pose a threat to the United States down the road? Do slaves ever revolt? With each percentage growth in our GDP, we become more exposed to foreign influence and destruction because of the debt we create both personally and nationally. The debt is created to pay the foreign low cost producers to do jobs that we won't. China is the premiere low cost producer in the world. Our exposure to China could be dangerous. They are a communist country that opposes democratic countries. It is an overpopulated state that could be reduced by half in a war and still have 600 million people left to enjoy the extra space even if they lost the war. No one will occupy China. It would be a logistic impossibility. They are building a stockpile of strategic weapons and developing a missile delivery system with the documents that were stolen during the Clinton administration (1999 Cox Congressional Report). Russia and America would be natural targets because of their natural resources. It would be logistically impossible for China to occupy Russia or America. But there are other ways of winning wars without having massive land battles.

China has already invaded America. They have us hooked on low cost labor. It's a narcotic for us. We are a country that is hooked on democracy and equality and willing to pay anything for it. With China, we can afford to have some people not work, we can afford some loss of productivity, and we can afford massive legal costs to micro manage the subtleties of race and gender relations with regard to work issues. China provides us with slave-like service so we can puff on the pipe of equality.

Will China do our bidding forever? Will they become jealous of our hegemony? If they choose an economic gambit before a military option, they'd hold some high cards. Suppose they raise their minimum wage that they charge America for piecework? That would be bad for our corporate profits and our inflation. It is hard to say at what point that type of move would be severely problematical to us. But the Chinese could just watch without incurring any military response. If we adjusted, they could raise the rates again and maybe boycott our goods and services. Maybe they would nationalize all those new American assembly plants that were built on Mainland China. Other countries would offer to China the goods we used to sell. China is a major creditor and contractor to America. At some point they could start a panic. China would be impacted also, but it would be relatively less of a burden because of a smaller group of beneficiaries in China. It is hard to say what would happen to the demeanor of the American population, but China would have shaken the U.S. without one shot being fired. Would democracy as we know it be at an end? Would rational economic planning and natural selection succeed the pipe dream of equality? Or would the government of equals take the form of socialism or communism? Would that succeed our democracy? All paradigm changes in government take place because of economic dislocation. With slave labor, China has put a down payment on the conquest of America. They worked while we borrowed money.

It all sounds farfetched. But when you build an economy and a society largely on someone else's work and borrowed money on top of that, one should ask oneself – what good can come out of those facts?

WHERE ARE THE MEEK?

ESSAY NINE

WHERE ARE THE MEEK?

RESONANCE

Let your spirit sing. Dance the space you feel you have. Compose, so others may dance and sing. These were the inspirational directives of the original three muses. They were the mythical daughters of the almighty Zeus and Mnemosyne, the goddess of memory. The muses were patronesses of music, dance and lyric poetry. They were part of the Greek pantheon.

Mnemosyne, the mother of the muses, was the Goddess of memory. Resonance is a form of memory – a recall by a feeling of echo. The resonance of the muses' inspiration lead to a personal composition. The music was there, in you, from the beginning. Maybe the pantheists deduced that music, dance and the ability to produce lyric poetry were a recall of the Olympian experience of the parents of the muses – Zeus and Mnemosyne. It is a sense of God-like serenity that is possible when one is happy to be oneself.

Zeus did not think much of man's presumptive claim to other God-like possessions. Read about Prometheus. Because of his theft of fire, he was chained to a rock where the crows perpetually plucked at his liver. The Greek translation of the name Prometheus is "to think ahead." Zeus indicated to mortals that their instinctive life, which included dance, music and lyricism, was more suitable. He implied "enjoy the moment."

Solon was a 6th century B.C. Greek lawgiver. He was a law giver of ancient Greece. There is no mention about the avoidance of the muses in the fragments of his life that have survived. But he did have something to say about Greek plays. He counseled his people not to attend too many plays. He instructed that life was to be lived, not vicariously or wistfully watched. Why did he draw a distinction between the patronage of muses and the creations of the Greek playwright? Aren't they both forms of entertainment?

Maybe the description, play, contains a clue to the difference. Play. Why the word play? Play in the sense of happy, in the sense of not real, in the sense of non-work? A thread in those alternatives is the sense of relief. Relief from what? Reality.

Amusing oneself with music, dance and lyricism are engaging acts. One can do them alone. They require an engagement of the individual to receive any benefits from the process. The making of music, the twirling of dance and the composition of lyric poetry require work. No work in – no joy out. There would be no sense of fulfillment if one did not sweat a little.

Plays are about passive involvement. People sit and watch. One might even use the time at the amphitheater to doze off or think about something entirely different. The chorus recites the storyline. The actors emote and talk from rote. The participation of the audience is limited to the buying of a ticket beforehand.

How does the plot of the play get from the stage to the audience and then made part of an audience's experience? It is someone else's words and actions. It is not the same as living through or earning an experience through effort. More broadly put, can anyone really be given something? Can an unearned position or a vicarious life be worthwhile?

Experience as defined by the dictionary describes an event that is the basis of knowledge.

How do we learn? We have to engage the subject personally, understand it and then it becomes ours. That has to be the way. Otherwise, any student that went to school and listened to a lecture would be immediately enriched. But we know that not to be the way of gaining knowledge.

Are plays a waste of time? No. Depending on the script and the actors, they can be entertaining and instructive. The organization of the theatrical experience and the lesson of the plot can deliver pleasure. But the evaluating of the play and its appreciation or non-appreciation requires knowledge gained beforehand – personal engagement in the real world. You have to come to the theatre already equipped with critical evaluation ability. Otherwise, you will be tossed ambivalently around by the script and the characters. I think Shakespeare, in one of his plays, has a character say, "The game is the thing." But one should know the difference between a game and something more important.

Here we are today, approximately 2600 years after Solon's caveats about watching too much entertainment and vicariously living one's life. Do these instructions have applications to the mainstream evening news?

Beware of anchormen on television who bring you the news and also want you to buy one of their sponsor's products – not necessarily in that order. If you don't buy, you won't see. Consumer throw away products are the usual impresario.

Does the philosophy of marketing consumer throw aways have a similarity in presenting the news?

For any communication to be successful – sales, news casting or play writing – the message has to be understood, both in language and in topic. Language speaks for itself, but the choice of the words has to be appropriate for the audience. The topic has to have a possibility of being of interest and something the audience can identify.

If the sponsor is laundry soap, the message by definition will be simple and directed to the lowest common denominator.

But now the news. The producers of the newscast have a good idea of the demographics of the viewing audience. The newscast will be aimed at the most typical viewer in words and subject matter that will be understood and familiar – no surprises or mental challenging. Stories that make the mediocre audience uncomfortable with their mediocre status will not be featured. Viewers are to be cultivated. There will be no losing market share. Even if it means not telling the real ramification of a story – the difference between the short term result and the possible long term ramifications. Therefore, the viewers will never be given anything new – at least ostensibly. Even 9/11, an unbelievable event in its simplicity but with far reaching complications, was treated as a validation of American foreign policy.

Some of the country questioned how we got so far off the path of our supposed global mission policy of peacekeeping to deserve this response.

The news media stood by their scripts – don't loose market share.

How should we get the news? How can we make ourselves aware of misinformation, omission or bad advice by the media?

Solon would have told us that it is too late to be educated by the news when it is presented. The presentation itself is the problem. The editors of the news have already determined what is to be shown and, by extension, what conclusions are to be drawn. It's a kind of poll taking in reverse. The pollsters can get any answer they want depending on to whom the questions are asked, what questions are asked, and the sequence of the questions. This leads respondents into logical traps. Solon would go on to advise that there is nothing new under the sun, even though 2600 years have passed. Only the date has changed. He would also say that one should live and learn from personal experience and maybe write about those experiences if one could not read to better advantage.

Compare your own life experiences with the evening news presentation – you draw your own conclusion. What resonates with you?

WHERE ARE THE MEEK?

ABOUT THE AUTHOR

"These buckets of water we are showering you with, just think of them as rain."

Barry Leonardini used this quote to answer the question, "Why did you write these essays?"

Mr. Leonardini was educated in the classics by the Jesuit Order at St. Ignatius Preparatory and for a time at the University of San Francisco. He was an honor student in Latin and Greek studies.

After a largely self-employed career for 30 years in the financial markets, he returned to the subject matter of his youth.

He continued to delve further in areas of philosophy, physics and anthropology.

He brings fresh, stimulating views and predictions regarding legal, financial and social issues. These engaging essays are based on his challenge to the thesis of laws that are based on the "equality of all."

The reading is easy, clear and thought-provoking and will stimulate conversation.

Mr. Leonardini has an unusually frank and succinct style.